SCHIRMER'S LIBRARY
OF MUSICAL CLASSICS

JOHANNES BRAHMS

Piano Works in Two Volumes

EDITED BY

E. v. SAUER

ISBN 0-7935-5233-8

G. SCHIRMER, Inc.

DISTRIBUTED BY
 HAL•LEONARD®
CORPORATION
7777 W. BLUEMOUND RD. P.O. BOX 13819 MILWAUKEE, WI 53213

CONTENTS

VOLUME I.

→ VOLUME II

Eight Piano Pieces

Capriccio.

Johannes Brahms, Op. 76 No 1. (1879.)

Printed in the U.S.A. by G. Schirmer, Inc.

Capriccio.

Op. 76 No 2.

Intermezzo.

Op. 76   Nº 3.

Grazioso.
Anmutig, ausdrucksvoll.

42738

Intermezzo.

Op. 76 № 4.

Allegretto grazioso.

Capriccio.

Agitato, ma non troppo presto.
Sehr aufgeregt, doch nicht zu schnell.

Op. 76 № 5.

Intermezzo.

Op. 76 Nº 6.

Andante con moto.
Sanft bewegt.

Intermezzo.

Moderato semplice.

Op. 76 № 7.

Capriccio.

Grazioso ed un poco vivace.
Anmutig lebhaft.

Two Rhapsodies

Agitato.

Op. 79 No 1. (1880.)

38

42738

Rhapsody

Molto passionato, ma non troppo Allegro.

Op. 79 № 2.

Fantasies
Capriccio.

Op. 116. № 1. *(1892)*

Intermezzo.

Op. 116. N⁰ 2.

Capriccio.

Allegro passionato.

Un poco meno Allegro.

Intermezzo.

Op. 116. No 4.

Intermezzo.

Andante con grazia ed intimissimo sentimento.

Op. 116. Nº 5.

42738

Intermezzo.

Op. 116. Nº 6.

Capriccio.

Op.116. № 7.

Three Intermezzi

Schlaf sanft, mein Kind, schlaf sanft und schön!
Mich dauert's sehr, dich weinen sehn.
(Schottisch. Aus Herders Volksliedern.)

Op. 117. Nᵒ 1. *(1892.)*

Andante moderato.

Un poco più Andante.

Intermezzo.

Andante non troppo e con molta espressione.

Op. 117. № 2.

42738

Intermezzo.

Six Piano Pieces
Intermezzo.

Allegro non assai, ma molto appassionato.

Op. 118 Nº 1 *(1893.)*

Intermezzo.

Op. 118 Nº 2.

Andante teneramente.

Ballade.

Allegro energico.

Op. 118 No 3.

Intermezzo.

Op. 118 N⁰ 4.

Allegretto un poco agitato.

Romance

Allegretto grazioso.

molto p e dolce sempre

p dolce

p leggiero

Intermezzo.

Op. 118 No 6.

Andante, largo e mesto.

42738

Four Piano Pieces

Intermezzo.

Op. 119 N⁰ 1. *(1893.)*

Adagio.

Intermezzo.

Andantino un poco agitato.

Op.119 № 2.

Andantino grazioso.

Intermezzo.

Op. 119 N⁰ 3.

Rhapsody

Op. 119 No 4.

Allegro risoluto.

Studies for Piano
Etude after Fr. Chopin   Study No. 1

Rondo after C. M. v. Weber   Study No. 2

*The Editor does not think Brahms' own fingering (lower fingering) useful for
public performance

*The Editor prefers to take the last 3 Sixteenths with the right hand

Presto after J. S. Bach   Study No. 3

(First arrangement)

Presto.

Presto after J. S. Bach   Study No. 4

(Second arrangement)

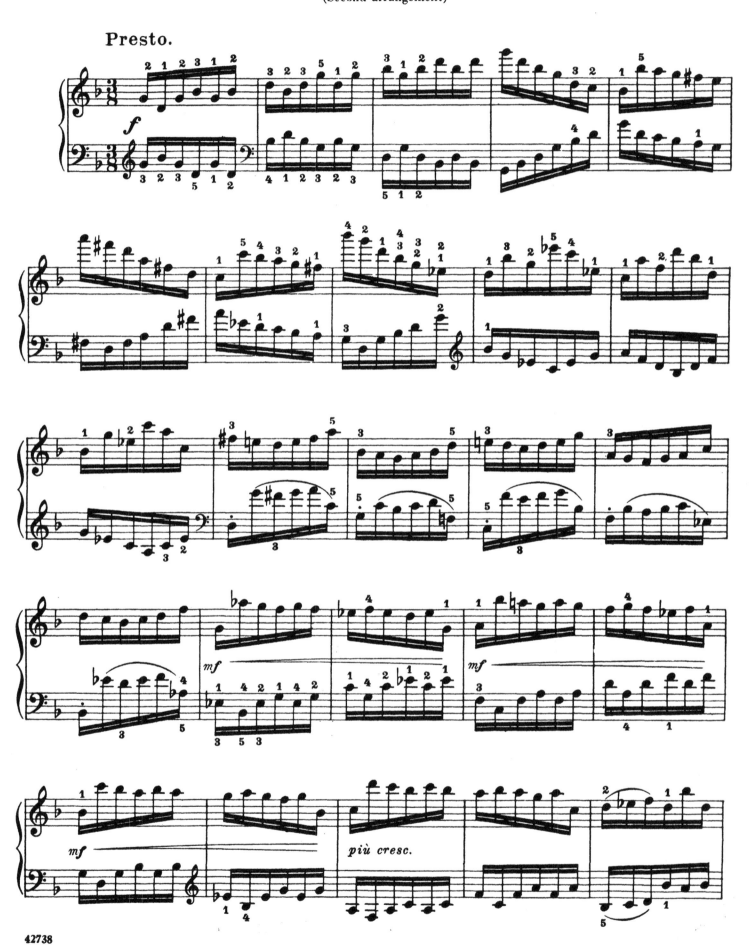

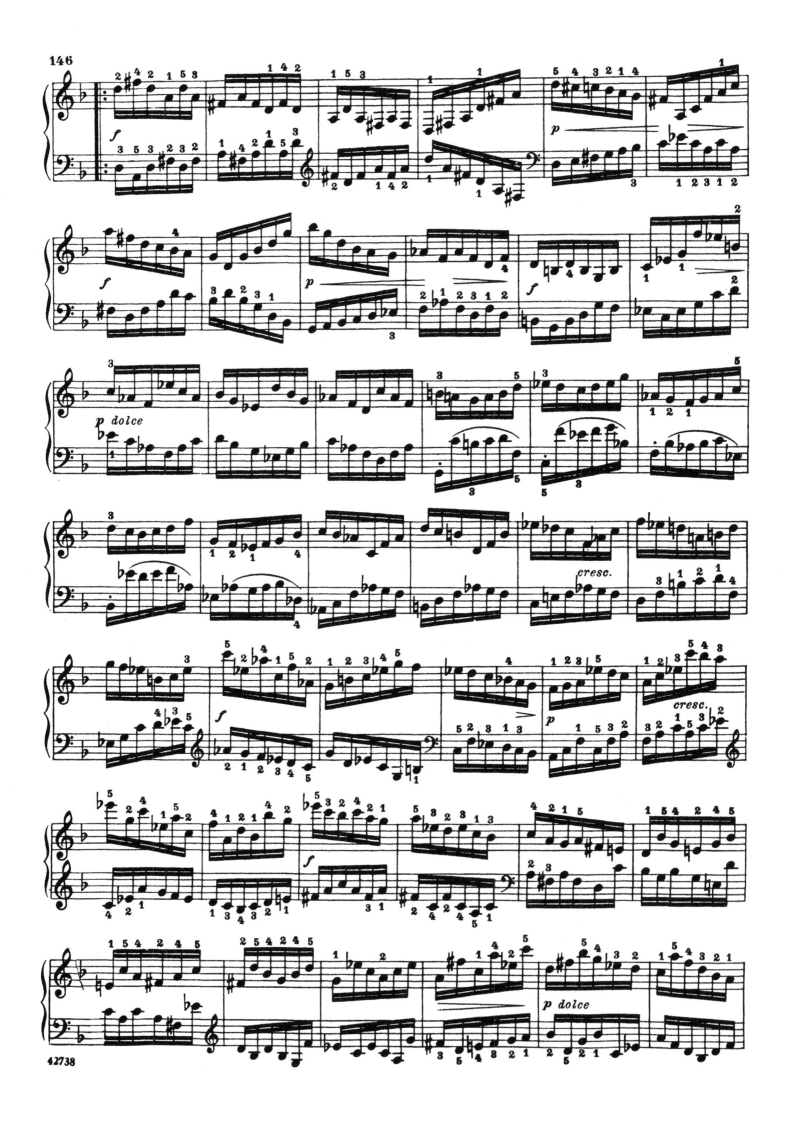

Chaconne by J. S. Bach   Study No. 5

(arranged for the left hand alone)

Moderato.

sempre *f e ben marc.*

ben marc.

f